# Face and Body Painting

# Face and Body Painting

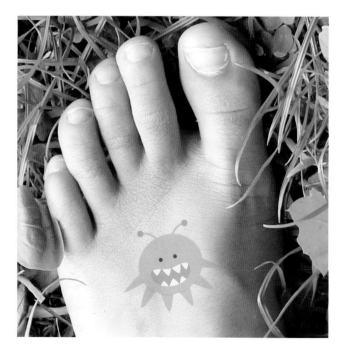
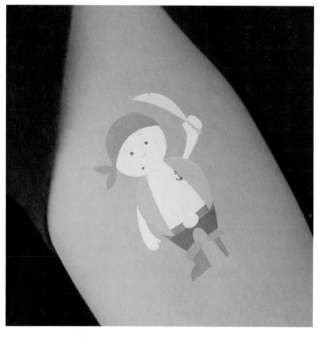

This edition published in 2014
By **SpiceBox™**
12171 Horseshoe Way
Richmond, BC
Canada V7A 4V4

First published in 2012
English text and design © SpiceBox 2013
Originally published in Spanish as "Maquillajes"
Spanish text and photographs copyright © 2004 Parramón Ediciones, S.A.
Ronda de Sant Pere, 5, 4ª planta
08010 Barcelona (España)

**ISBN 10:** 1-77132-187-3
**ISBN 13:** 978-1-77132-187-7

CEO & Publisher: Ben Lotfi
Author: Pilar Amaya
Editorial: Ania Jaraczewski
Creative Director: Garett Chan
Art Director: Christine Covert
Design, Photography & Illustration: Charmaine Muzyka
Production: James Badger, Mell D'Clute
Sourcing: Janny Lam, Desmond Hung
Photography: Nos & Soto
Special thanks to the models: Bryan Ormandy, Selma Dzumhura,
Jennifer Blanco, Cameron Attwell

For more SpiceBox products and information, visit our website:
**www.spiceboxbooks.com**

Manufactured in China

3 5 7 9 10 8 6 4 2

# Contents

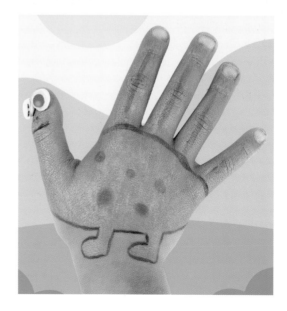

# Introduction

It's always an adventure to become someone – or something – else for a day. Whether it's for Halloween, a birthday party or some other special occasion, the magic of transforming yourself through face makeup, body art and temporary tattoos is a great way to create a whole new you!

In this book, you'll find fun and original makeup ideas that will let you transform yourself into animals, fantastic landscapes, objects and much more. If you want to have a fun time with your friends and family, or at school, carefully follow these simple step-by-step instructions and you will see that face and body painting is much easier than you might think.

# You Are the Canvas!

Getting dressed up and putting on makeup is a great way to mark special times in your life, or just to have fun. People around the world have been using body art for centuries to celebrate and entertain: from tribal ceremonies to weddings and theater performances.

Looking different than you usually do is fun and exciting! And it's great that there are lots of ways that you can change your appearance for just a few hours, so you can go back to being you afterward!

Body paints and temporary tattoos are perfect to try out different looks, surprise your friends and celebrate at parties. They are easy to wash off, so you can try out different designs and always look forward to your next disguise.

Use these projects as inspiration, and then try out your own fantastical creations! Get together with friends and have a fun face-painting party. Be creative and use your new skills to turn yourself into anything you want to become!

# Prehistoric Makeup

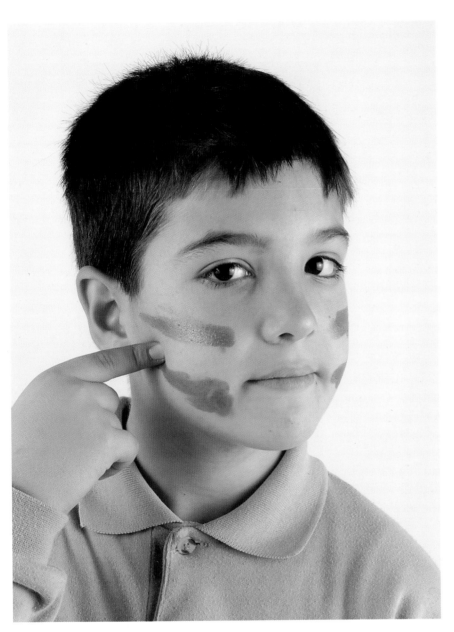

In your palm, mix a little earth with water. Use the mud to make stripes on your face. This is the way that humans first used face painting to camouflage themselves and change their appearance.

Did you know that the art of makeup is very old? Prehistoric cave people used it to prepare for ceremonies and battles, painting themselves with earth, charcoal, animal blood and plant dyes. With this early makeup they also camouflaged themselves for hunting. As time passed, people continued to experiment with different vegetable and mineral sources for colors, as well as with the waxes, fats and liquids to mix them with for easy application to the face and body.

# Become an 18th Century Courtier!

The art of makeup has a long history. In ancient Egypt, women began to paint their lips with a colorant made from red ocher and iron oxide. In religious and burial rituals it was important to create masks on the deceased, painting their faces with vibrant ceremonial colors for the journey to the afterlife. Paintings of these masks can be found on the walls of tombs.

The art of makeup was an important element in the cultures and traditions of other great empires, such as those of the Greeks and Romans, and was often rich with symbolism and meaning.

By the eighteenth century, beauty and class became the main reasons people used makeup. It was no longer used symbolically; instead the goals were to hide signs of aging, acne and disease, and to look wealthy by not having the suntanned skin of the field laborer. It became fashionable for both men and women to whiten their faces with powder, which had the effect of making everyone look the same.

Today, there are plenty of makeup products to beautify and enhance the way we look, including eye shadow and liners, lipsticks, blushes, bronzers, concealers and foundation — makeup is now part of our everyday lives.

To get the look of an 18th-century courtier, whiten your face with flour, darken your eyebrows with eye pencil, use red lipstick on your lips, and finish up with rouge circles on your cheeks.

# Makeup: An Expressive Tool

Makeup is also an important and useful way to help you express the personality of another character. In the world of theater and film, makeup is an essential tool for actors to get into character and make their performances more believable. With the artful use of makeup, you can achieve incredible results: a child can look like an old man, or a small nose can become huge. A talented makeup artist can completely transform an actor into a monster or alien! Makeup is a mask painted directly on your face; when used with body language and voice, it can completely transform you into another person. Magic!

# Let's Paint Our Faces!

Let's have some fun! Any occasion will do, whether it's for a party, celebrating a birthday or going to a carnival. Whether you're dressing up for Halloween or a performance, or simply spending a special day with friends or surprising your family, face painting frees you to express yourself however you want.

## Concentration

The art of makeup requires concentration. You need to be calm, and have a positive attitude and lots of patience, especially for adding small details with a brush. Pay attention to how an adult paints your face and note their patience and concentration.

## Observation

Look in the mirror and look at your face and expression. Does the natural curve of your lips show joy or sorrow? The eyebrows are extremely expressive – can you make yours look determined, puzzled, questioning?

## Creativity

Thanks to the magic of makeup, you can become any character or thing you can imagine. Start by looking at the world around you for face-painting inspiration – nature is always an interesting source of ideas. Just add your own imagination and creativity to come up with a wonderful design. If you are inspired one sunny day by a butterfly flitting between flowers, why not transform your face into a fantastic and elegant butterfly using your favorite colors and your own special design for the wings?

The amazing effects achievable with makeup let you create all sorts of awesome characters – try turning yourself into a super-intelligent robot that can talk just like a human! Or turn yourself into an animated cell phone or grand piano.

Holidays provide wonderful reasons for dressing up! Halloween, Carnival, Mardi Gras and the Mexican Day of the Dead are occasions to paint your face and wear a costume.

# Be Original!

Transform your face into a living skull, a scary monster or a cute and quirky elf.

But if you really want to surprise your friends and family with something unique, you can turn your face into a beautiful landscape or perhaps create a scene of a sailing ship at sea, guided to the shore by a lighthouse.

Imagine that your face is a continuation of your favorite shirt. Choose a top with a pattern that you can extend onto your face. How clever!

# Materials

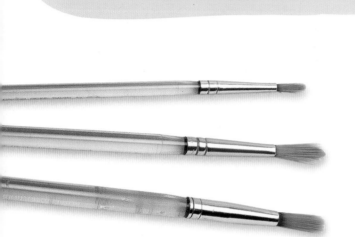

Preparing for a special event can be as fun as the celebration itself. We designed these projects for children 8 years and up to do on their own with adult supervision.

There is a broad range of face-painting makeup on the market, and it can range in price and quality, from the inexpensive to pricey professional products. To find out if you enjoy face painting and want to pursue it further, we recommend starting with simple techniques and common materials. These will give great results while you develop your skills.

## Paints and Brushes

For the demonstrations used in the book, all of the makeup used is water-based. Face paint can be found in toy, craft and costume stores, and is sold in bottles, cakes, crayons and pencils. Any of these will work for the techniques used in the book. Make sure you only use paints that are for face and body painting. Water-based paints can be applied directly to the face as long as you don't have any greasy cream on your face that would repel it. Non-toxic face and body paints won't damage the skin and are easily removed with soap and water. It's always a good idea to choose products that are labelled hypoallergenic to avoid an allergic reaction. If you have any doubts, perform a skin patch test before using them.

In some cases, we use standard cosmetics, such as eye shadow, lipstick and eyeliner. Make sure you have permission before using anyone else's makeup! Eventually, you may find you want to buy some makeup of your own to keep in your costume kit.

Make sure brushes are soft and don't feel scratchy on your skin. Start with three sizes of small pointed brushes, ranging from very fine, to fine, to medium, plus one flat, wide one for painting bigger areas.

You should always have a container for water to wash your brushes in. Change the water frequently so your colors stay bright. A few other handy household items are tissues, cotton swabs and sponges. For coloring the ears, sponges are better than brushes because they are less likely to drip paint into your ear.

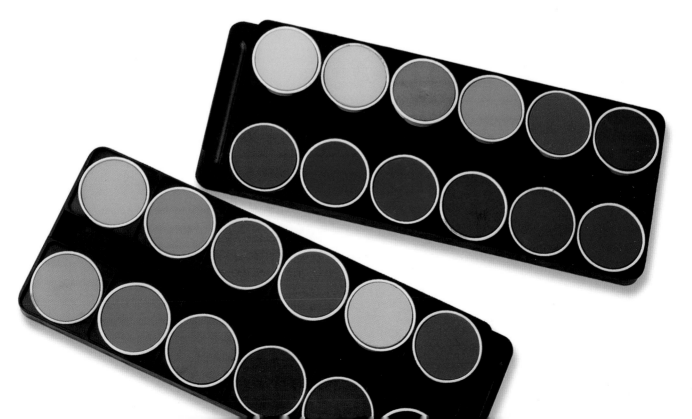

# Other Useful Tools

Although you can achieve excellent results with just paint, a few other supplies can add that something special. Glitter can give a beautiful shine to makeup. Mix glitter with hair gel or buy ready-made glitter gel.

Don't forget to think about the right hairstyle for each makeup design. It's good to have a comb, brush, styling wax, hair spray and gel on hand to allow you to create some cool styles to suit your makeup. A neat makeup trick is to style your hair with gel, and while it is still a bit damp, stroke on some paint to add streaks.

Temporary colored hair sprays sold in drugstores, craft stores or costume shops are also very useful for quick and easy hair color. Just make sure to always protect your eyes with a paper towel or a cloth. Both the paint and sprays are easily removed with soap and water.

# Final Tips Before You Start

- Set up your work area so that everyone can comfortably work on the makeup for the duration of the project. The person getting made up should be sitting in a comfortable chair. The person applying the makeup will want a table to hold supplies. A mirror and excellent lighting are essential for watching your character develop!

- Paper towels and tissues are handy for wiping and cleanup.

- Water-based face paints may need several applications to achieve the richness of color you want.

- When you want to paint one color on top of another, make sure the first color has dried completely so the colors don't mix. To speed up the drying process, you can use a handheld hairdryer on the coolest setting, making sure you first tell your model to close his or her eyes, and to let you know if it's too hot or irritating.

# Drawing Your Ideas

Art is all around us, and we can take inspiration from many sources – theater, books, cartoons, movies or paintings – and the process of creating your own special design can be exciting. Pay attention to the things that interest you and use them as the starting point for your project. Use your imagination and sketch out ideas that come to mind using the template on the next page. You may want to photocopy or scan it so that you have extra copies for working on your ideas. When you've made a design you like, use your drawing as a reference guide for your face painting.

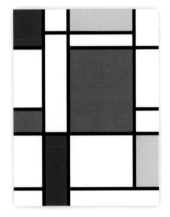   

## Art

Mondrian was an influential 20th century painter. A fabulous face-painting design could be based on his distinctive geometric style. Look at art for inspiration.

## Animals

Many of the projects in this book demonstrate how you can camouflage your own features when you paint over them with a striking design, like the beak and colors of a lovebird.

## Performing Arts

Whether it's opera, ballet, children's theater or pantomime, theatrical costumes are amazing! Here is a face design based on Pagliacci, the opera about a sad clown.

## Comics

Look through comic books to find a superhero costume that appeals to you. You can copy it or individualize it by changing the colors and shapes, or combine the costumes of several heroes.

**Use this template to sketch out your face-painting ideas**

# Jungle Tiger

## Materials

- paints: orange, white, brown, yellow & black
- makeup sponge
- brushes: medium & fine

Animal costumes and makeup are popular at parties. How fun would it be to transform yourself into a ferocious tiger or a cute kitten for a little while? Here's your chance to become one of the big cats and give a giant roar to announce your arrival.

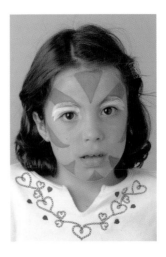

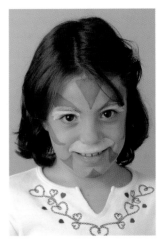

**1.** For the base of this tiger makeup, apply an all-over layer of orange face paint with a damp sponge.

**2.** When the entire face is covered, paint the eyelids white with a medium brush. Paint up and over the eyebrows to make the eyelids appear larger.

**3.** Around the face, paint several light brown stripes to look like the markings on a tiger.

**4.** For the animal's snout, cover the space between the nose and the upper lip (the mustache area) with yellow paint.

**Tip:** To apply a foundation of paint over the entire face, first wet a sponge and squeeze most of the water out. Dab the soft, damp sponge into the paint to pick up the color. Using a sponge to apply paint in broad strokes is easier than using a paintbrush.

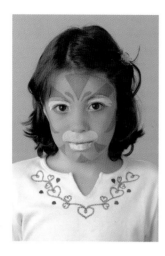

**5.** Now paint the bottom lip white, extending it a bit below the lip and narrower than the upper lip. Make a few little brush strokes of paint below the lip to look like fur. Add small brown markings on the forehead above the eyes.

**6.** Taking extra care to work safely around the eyes, outline the eyes in brown and make black spots on the mustache area for the whisker pores.

**7.** To finish the makeup, paint the tip of the nose black, extending a thin black line down to the lip.

# Variations

**Cat:** You might prefer a cat that isn't quite so wild! Using care around the eyes, paint an orange spot around one eye, and a brown one around the other. Paint the nose, mustache area and eyelids white, then paint the tip of the nose black. Use a thin brush and black paint to add dots and whiskers in the mustache area, and paint a line down the center to the upper lip. To finish off, slowly and carefully outline the eyes in black, add black brows and paint the lips gray. This cat is ready to meow!

**Bengal Tiger:** For a more exotic feline look, how about that other great cat, the Bengal tiger? With a wide flat brush, cover the entire forehead, mustache area and below the bottom lip with white. Sponge yellowy orange onto the rest of the face. Paint the nose brown, and when that dries, paint black on the tip. Continue using a fine brush loaded with black paint for the markings over the eyes, the stripes on the cheeks and those extending from the corners of the mouth. Finish off with a few whiskers, and prepare to scare with this terrific tiger!

# Seascape

## Materials

- paints: white, yellow, red, black & different blues
- brush: fine
- makeup sponge

There are many famous paintings of landscapes, but have you ever thought of using your own face as a canvas for a beautiful picture? Why not start with a seascape featuring a lighthouse guiding a ship home over the storm-tossed sea? If are pleased with the results, you can use your imagination and creativity to create more landscape designs.

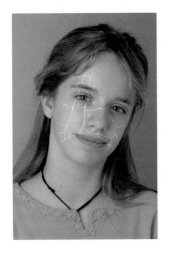

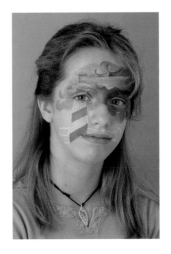

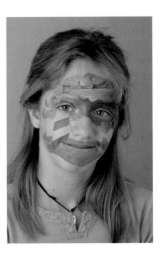

**1.** Before starting to paint, use a thin brush and white paint to draw an outline of the seascape over your face. Start with the outline of the lighthouse, add a line for the sky, a middle line for the stormy sea and a bottom line for the beach.

**2.** Paint in the lighthouse with red and yellow. Don't forget to continue the picture over your eyelid so that it is a complete lighthouse when you close your eyes. Use care when painting around the eyes.

**3.** To create three different blues for your seascape, first use the blue as it comes, then make a dark blue by adding a little black, and a third blue by mixing blue with white. When the sky is dry, add some gray stormy clouds. Use white to paint the lighthouse's beacon of light shining across the sky.

**4.** For the waves of the sea, pick a different blue than the one you used for the sky – perhaps one that has a bit of green mixed into it. Paint the sea, then paint a yellow beach on your chin and bottom lip.

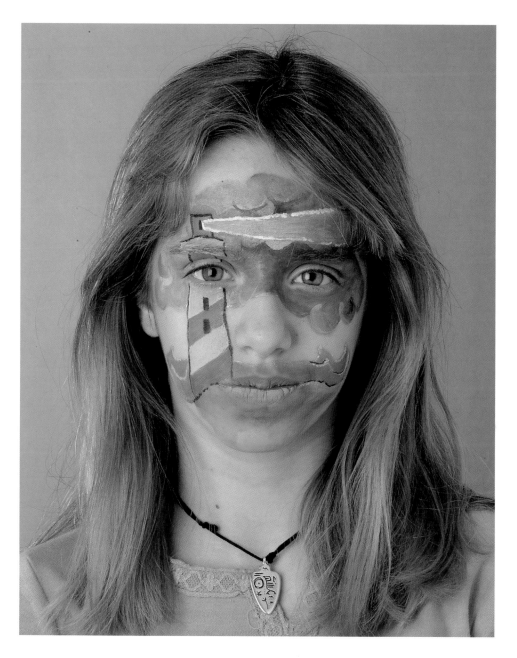

**5.** Finish the details of your painting with a fine brush and black paint, outlining the lighthouse and adding windows.

**Tip:** As water-based paint dries, your face may feel tighter. It feels a bit odd at first, but once the paint is dry, you'll be able to move your face without fear of the paint cracking or flaking off.

# Grand Piano

## Materials

- paint colors: white, black & gray
- brushes: fine, medium & large flat
- hair gel

How about transforming your face into the keyboard of a piano? It's so easy to do, you'll want to paint all your friends as musical instruments so you can walk around together as a human orchestra!

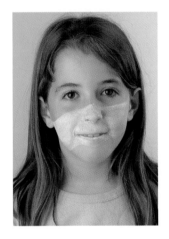

**1.** With a flat brush, paint a slanted white stripe across the lower half of your face, continuing the stripe over your mouth and nose.

**2.** When the white stripe has dried, use a fine brush to paint over it with black vertical lines to make piano keys. Paint the first line down the center of your nose, and then space the remaining keys out evenly along the keyboard.

**3.** Now, using a thicker brush, paint the black keys. Remember that black piano keys are arranged in alternating groups of two and three with two white keys between each group.

**4.** Use gray paint for the shadow beneath the keyboard.

**5.** Take the thin brush again to paint black musical symbols and notes over the rest of the face. Comb back your hair with gel and put on a fancy bow tie made out of tissue paper. Cue the music, maestro!

**Tip:** It's always a good idea to work in front of a large mirror so your model can see how the painting is progressing. This is especially helpful when your model is very young and prone to fidgeting.

# Nibbly Mouse

## Materials

- paints: light & dark gray, black & white
- brushes: fine & medium
- water-soluble crayon: gray

An adorable little mouse can get into every nook and cranny to look for cheese and other tasty treats! With this simple makeup you can turn into one of these tiny creatures, but when you see a cat, scurry off and hide!

  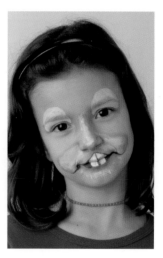 

**1.** With the water-soluble crayon, paint ovals on the eyelids and eyebrows. Slow down and think about working safely when painting around the eyes

**2.** Use dark gray paint to cover the entire nose, upper lip and the corners of the cheeks.

**3.** Draw the mouse's upper lip and teeth over your own upper lip using the fine brush and black paint. Extend the mouse's teeth down over your own lips. Use white paint to fill in the teeth. Under the lower lip, paint in a small gray and white patch of fur.

**4.** With a fine paintbrush, paint in black details, such as the whiskers, nose and eyebrows. With light gray paint, add hairs on the forehead. Now all you need to do is put your hair up into two cute little pigtails that look like mouse ears, and you are ready to scamper off in search of some tasty cheese!

**Tip:** Painting the teeth is the most complicated step of this design. You have to keep your lips closed in a relaxed position, and not move them until the teeth are completely painted in. The teeth need to line up on the top and bottom lip.

# Spring Print

## Materials

- paints: white, pink, fuchsia, green, blue, orange, yellow
- brushes: selection from fine to thick
- water-soluble crayons in all colors

This design will ensure you have the most unique look at any party. Find a shirt with a great print and extend the pattern to your face. In the following instructions, you'll see how we built on the printed top shown in the photograph. When you do your own, start by studying your shirt and deciding how to best continue the pattern.

  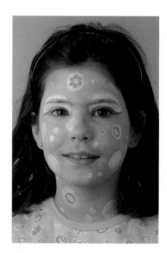 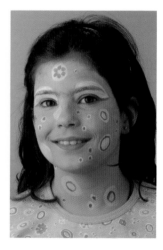

**1.** Paint white all over both eyelids and eyebrows.

**2.** Use a sponge to cover the rest of your face and neck with thick pink paint. Try to match the color as closely as possible to the main color of the top.

**3.** Use a medium brush to paint white spots of various sizes across your face. Inside each spot, use pink to paint the flowers and other patterns from the print.

**4.** Now add blue to the flowers, dots and rings inside the spots.

**Tip:** The paint should not be too thick or too thin. Add water until you have a creamy consistency that is easy to spread.

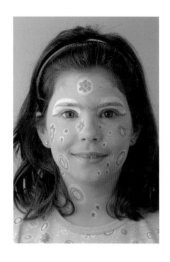

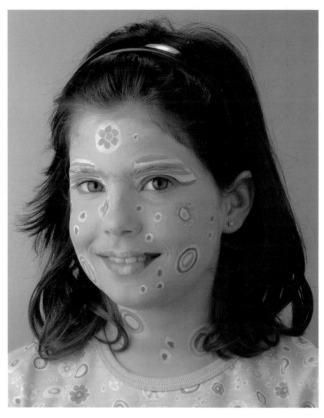

**5.** With a fine brush, Add in details in green, yellow, orange, pink and light blue using paints and water-soluble crayons.

**6.** Pull your hair back with a hair band so you can paint your face right up to the hairline. Paint rainbow colors over your eyes and lips.

# Variations

**Stripes:** Every shirt has a different pattern, so look at each pattern for inspiration for your hair and makeup. A striped shirt is loads of fun to copy onto your face, and is super simple to do. Extend the blue sleeves up your neck and the side of your face, then fill in the rest of your face with horizontal stripes of various thicknesses in pink, red, yellow, green and blue. It will be easier to do these lines with water-soluble crayons that are slightly dampened. You may want to paint your lips blue for a fun contrast.

**Flowers:** To continue the floral pattern of this shirt, you'll need a little imagination. Load a sponge with light blue paint and spread the color over the face. With a fine brush loaded with dark blue, outline flowers and leaves based on the shirt pattern, but vary the sizes. Fill these outlines in with red, white or the same light blue.

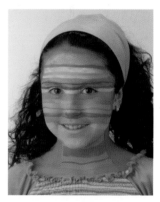

# Frankenstein

## Materials

- paint: light & dark green, dark gray, black & silver
- brushes: medium & fine
- makeup sponge
- hair gel

Monsters abound in scary games and movies. Not only will you have loads of fun transforming yourself with this frightening makeup, but you'll get to go out and scare all your friends afterward. Mwa ha ha!

  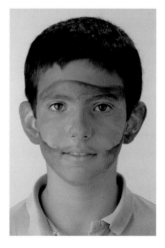 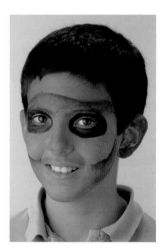

**1.** Wet a sponge, then squeeze all the water out. Dab the soft, damp sponge in paint to color your whole face green.

**2.** Paint your ears a slightly darker shade, staying to the outer edges. Don't get the paint inside your ear.

**3.** Using a medium brush and dark gray paint, draw wavy lines across your forehead and cheeks, as though you have the lumpy, misshapen head of a monster. Smooth the lines out a bit with a damp brush or sponge. Blending will make the makeup look more natural.

**4.** Make your eyes look deep-set and scary by painting around them with very dark green paint. Be careful and conscious of safety when painting around the eyes.

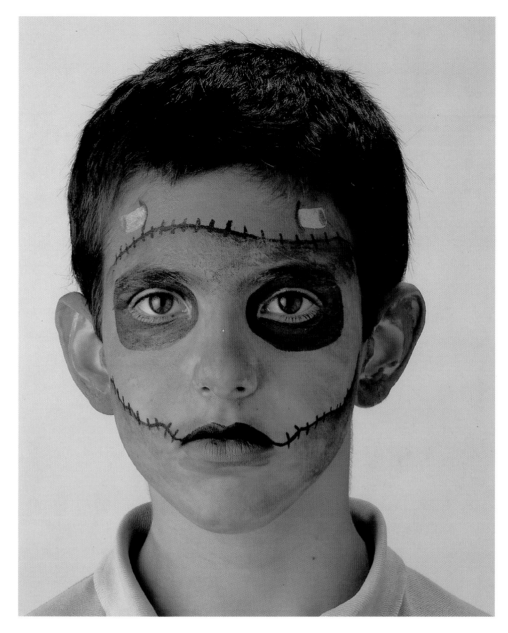

**5.** With a fine brush and black paint, draw scars on your face. Draw stitches across the lines you painted on your forehead in step 3. Paint silver screws to look like they're coming out of each of your temples.

# Variation

**Monster:** Monsters are fantastic and are as varied as your imagination can make them. Be creative and think of other monsters that you would enjoy portraying! You can paint your entire face a grayish-green color, adding gray wrinkles on your forehead and dark circles under your eyes. Paint brown blotches above your eyes and along your jawline, continuing around your mouth. A great touch is to paint your lips a dark color and add some nasty white fangs coming out of your mouth, above your top lip. Finish your new monster makeup off by spraying or painting your hair green! Use a well-ventilated area and cover your eyes when using a spray.

# Cell Phone

## Materials

- paints: white, purple, silver, yellow, blue, red, green & black
- brush: fine
- hair gel

Other inspiration for designs that create striking results can be ordinary household items. Look around you and see an everyday object that can be turned into a cool face painting. But beware — if you paint a cell phone on your face, someone might want to make a call or send a text!

 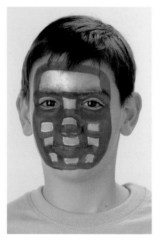 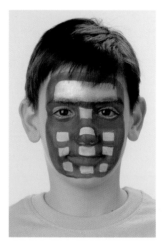 

**1.** The first thing to do is to use a fine brush to paint a white rectangle with rounded edges to cover most of your face. Draw a large rectangular area for the phone display and small squares for all of the buttons on the keypad. You can use your eyelids for the on and off buttons.

**2.** Paint the body of the phone purple. Fill in the screen with silver paint.

**3.** Paint the nine number keys yellow.

**4.** Add blue to the center button on the bridge of your nose. If your bangs get in the way, you can style your hair back and off your face with some hair gel.

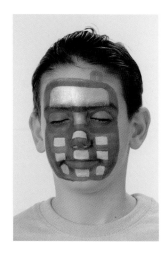

**5.** With your eyes closed, paint the eyelids completely — one red ("off") and the other green ("on"). Remember, don't open your eyes until the paint has completely dried.

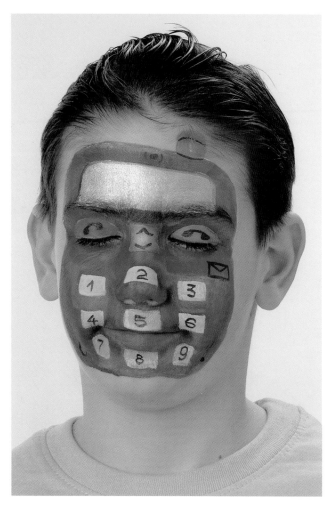

**6.** Use a fine brush and black paint to finish off your phone. With the tip of you brush, carefully paint the numbers on the keys, on and off buttons, and the scroll button between the eyes.

Now you are ready to start taking calls!

# Variation

**Puzzle:** There are many objects around us every day that can be turned into fun and funky face-painting designs. For instance, instead of a mobile phone, you could turn your face into a puzzle. It's simple: divide the face into six approximately equal parts by drawing three vertical and two horizontal lines. With a fine brush, draw the curved edges of the puzzle pieces. Paint five of the pieces different colors but leave one piece unpainted. Draw a pale line of shadow around the edge to make it look like the puzzle is incomplete. You could cut and paint a piece of cardboard in the shape of the missing piece, and pretend you are about to finish off the puzzle on your face!

# Robot

## Materials

• paint: black, silver & gold
• brushes: fine & medium
• glitter gel
• silver hair spray

If you are able to get your hands on some gold and silver paint, you can create a wonderful metallic effect. While transforming yourself into a friendly robot, practice your robot voice. Coupled with robotic moves, you'll be a great success at any party!

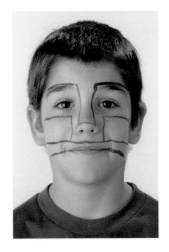

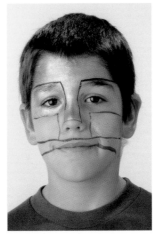

**1.** With a fine brush and black paint draw the shapes of the metal plates on the face of your robot. You can draw lines coming from the corners of the mouth, above the eyebrows and on the nose and cheeks.

**2.** Fill in the forehead and the nose sections with silver paint. Also paint around one eye and the square on the opposite cheek. It's important to remember to take special care to not get paint in your eyes.

**3.** Now fill in around the other eye and the square on the opposite cheek with black paint.

**4.** Use gold on the bottom of the nose and the rectangle on the chin. Fill in the rest of your face with silver.

**Tip:** If you spray-paint your hair, you must close your eyes and shield your face. Consider holding a sheet of paper over your face while someone else sprays your hair. It's not safe to spray-paint your face, but spray paint can be used safely on your arms or hands.

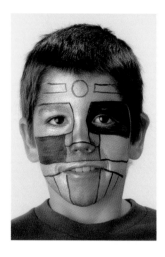

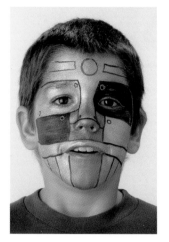

**5.** Using a thin brush loaded with black paint, retrace the black lines and add in details for your robot face, such as rectangles on either side on the forehead and a circle in the middle.

**6.** Draw some rivets on each metal plate. Use black paint when painting over silver and gold pieces, and silver paint when adding rivets to the black areas.

**7.** Use silver hair spray paint for your hair and wear a silver headband with toy bolts attached. To add shine to your robot, apply some glitter gel. Put on the bolts and bust out your best robot moves!

# Variation

**Medieval Armor:** Another metallic face-painting design that looks fantastic is medieval armor.

You can achieve this look using the same black, silver and gold paints. The only real difference to the design is in drawing the outline of the helmet. Use the silver spray paint on your arms and hands to create your knight's gauntlets.

# Butterfly Mask

## Materials

- paints: pink, violet, green, orange, red & silver
- brushes: medium & fine
- water-soluble crayon: white
- glitter gel

Instead of painting your entire face, these beautiful butterfly wings wrap around your eyes to create a mask. Just draw in the shape of a butterfly and add colors that go with your dress. You'll be the belle of the ball!

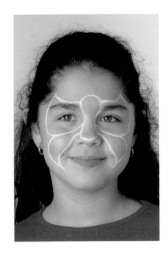   

**1.** Dampen the water-soluble white crayon and draw the outline of the butterfly's body over your face. Draw the body along your nose and the wings on either side. Try to make both sides symmetrical.

**2.** Paint the body of the butterfly with a mix of pink and purple.

**3.** Now, paint the two upper wings with pretty teal or blue paint. Take special care when outlining the eye area so you don't get paint in your eyes!

**4.** Use a blend of orange and red paints to fill in the lower parts of the wings.

**5.** Once the painted areas are dry, paint over your white outline with silver paint using a medium brush. Paint two silver antennae on your forehead.

Add glamor by applying some glitter gel on various parts of the butterfly. Gorgeous!

# Scary Skull

## Materials

- paints: brown, dark yellow, black & white
- brushes: fine & medium
- water-soluble crayon: white

If you want to scare your friends, you can transform your face into a white skull. Put on some scary music and move around like a skeleton that has come to life!

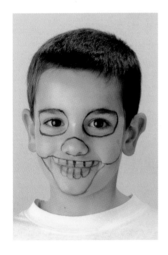 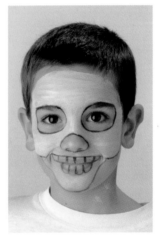  

**1.** With a fine brush and dark brown paint, trace two circles around your eyes and the end of your nose. Also draw a line along your cheeks where your jaws meet. Outline your "teeth" with black squares along your lips.

**2.** Mix white, dark yellow and a tiny bit of brown to get a cream color. Use this to paint your entire face, except inside the circles and squares you made in step 1.

**3.** Use the medium brush and black paint to fill in the eye area and the tip of the nose to get the look of the empty eye sockets and the absent nose of a skull. Slow down and think about working safely when painting around the eyes.

**4.** Paint the squares of the teeth with white paint.

**5.** Use the fine brush and black and brown paints for outlining the teeth. You can also add small jagged lines and dots of a darker cream paint to make it look like the skull is cracked and broken in places.

**Tip:** Paint your hair white and widen your eyes — the effect is terrifying! To paint your hair white, wet the tip of a water-soluble crayon and run it gently over your hair. It's easy to shampoo out.

# Fantasy Fish

## Materials

- paints: blue-gray, blue, lilac, silver, light green, dark red
- brushes: fine & medium
- makeup sponge
- glitter gel
- hair gel

Fantasy is an essential ingredient of any costume. Why don't you try to imagine a fish like you've never seen and transform yourself! The glimmering colors and unique patterns make a beautiful undersea creature.

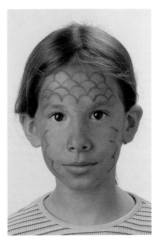

**1.** Use a damp sponge dipped in blue-gray paint to cover the entire face. Don't forget your neck and ears.

**2.** Start by framing your face with scales. Use a fine brush loaded with blue paint to draw in three rows of semicircles across your forehead. On the sides of your face, paint vertical rows of semicircles.

**3.** Paint inside each of the scales with stripes of purple and silver.

**4.** Finish filling in the scales with light green mixed with silver.

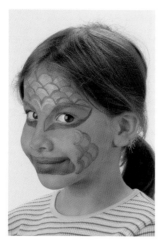

**5.** Make safety your priority when working around the eyes in this and other steps. Draw an oval shape around each eye, painting the top half green and the bottom half blue. Keep your eyes closed until the paint dries.

**6.** With red paint, color on and around your lips to make them look much larger. Point the corners of your mouth down to look more like a fish's mouth.

**7.** Finally, add glitter gel to your lips and to your eyelids. The glitter will sparkle like droplets of water on your scales.

# Variation

**Wise Gnome:** Other fantasy creatures are great inspiration for face painting, including this cute gnome. You only need to paint on a white bushy beard, moustache and thick overgrown eyebrows. Add some rosy red blush to the apples of your cheeks and at the tip of your nose. The most detailed part of this design is in the gnome's eyeglasses. First draw in the frame of the glasses as though they are sitting at the end of your nose. Paint the frames in gold, with a very fine black line on the lower edge of the frame to create a shadow. Make small dots for the screws, and fill in the lenses of the glasses with light gray. Give the appearance of light by adding fine white lines. Tie a red scarf over your hair and you are ready to pop out of the forest!

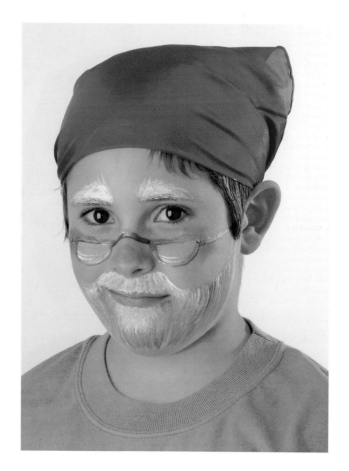

# Girl or Boy?

## Materials

- paint: black & brown
- brush: thick
- sponge
- blue eye shadow
- blush
- black eyeliner
- red lipstick
- mascara
- hair gel

Do you want to confuse your friends? Are you a man? Are you a woman? Who are you? By painting one half of your face with female features, and the other half with a beard and moustache, it'll be hard to tell! You could even put on a show by singing both parts of a duet!

**1.** Start by painting the male half of the face. To do this, lightly dab the beard area with a sponge dipped in thinned black paint.

**2.** When your shadow has dried, mix brown with a little black and use the thick brush to paint half a moustache and beard. With the same colors, paint in one thick eyebrow.

**3.** Now create the female half of the face by applying eye shadow and red blush to the cheek.

**4.** Paint half of your lips with red lipstick, add mascara to your lashes, and outline your eyes with black eyeliner.

**Tip:** For the male half, slick your hair back with hair gel, pinning it over to the female side where you can leave it hanging free. Add an earring to the female side to complete the look. What a cool effect!

 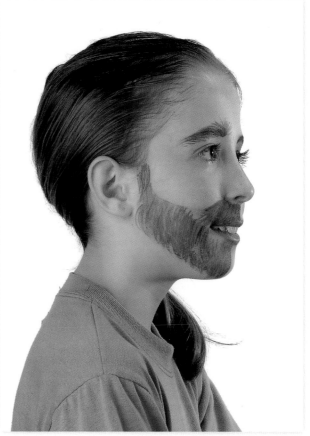

**Tip:** For the woman's makeup, you can use regular cosmetics. Ask an adult to show you how to properly apply makeup so you don't damage it or get it in your eyes.

# Tips & Tricks

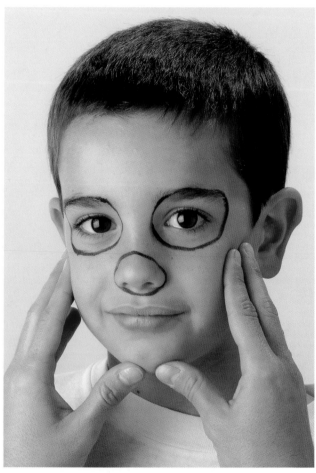

## Covering Your Face with a Single Base Color

To successfully paint a solid base color, you should use a makeup sponge or fine-textured natural sponge. First wet the sponge with water and wring it out before dipping it in the color and wiping it over the face. This method allows you to apply the paint in smooth strokes. Be extra careful when applying the paint around the eyes and ears. If you wish to darken the color, wait for the first layer of paint to dry before applying another coat.

## Locate Your Own Bones Before Painting the Skull

For all makeup, it's important to understand the bone structure of the model. For the skull makeup, it's especially important because you want to follow the model's eye socket and jawline for realistic proportions. To do this, use the tips of your fingers to feel the face and find the parts of the skull beneath the skin.

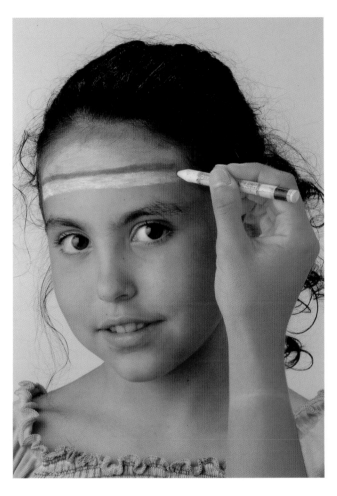

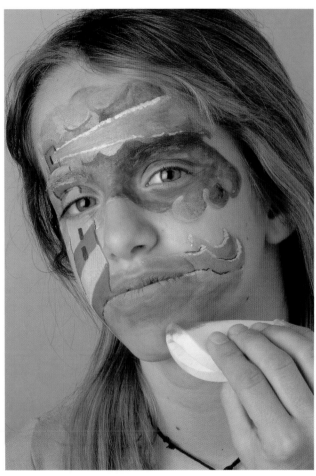

## Drawing Straight Lines

Use water-soluble crayons for straight lines. They go on smoothly and are easier to use than paintbrushes, which require a steady, even hand. Just wet the tip of the crayon and draw directly on the skin.

## Covering a Small Area With a Base Color

When you wish to fill a smaller area such as the forehead or chin with a base color, you can still use a sponge. Fold a flat sponge in half or pinch a small section of the natural sponge to paint with more precision and to work around corners. Again, if you wish to darken the area, wait until the first layer is dry before adding additional layers.

# Tips & Tricks

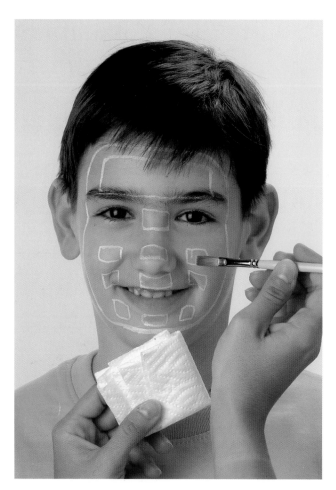

## Erasing Mistakes

Face painting works best if you first outline the design with pale lines before filling in the color. That way you can easily re-wet the line and dab away small mistakes. Gently pat and dab with clean tissue or paper towel to clean and dry the area you are erasing.

## Painting Above Your Eyes

Water-soluble crayons also are very useful for painting above your eyes and over the eyebrows. Dampen the crayons with water before painting so they'll soften and glide easily on the more delicate areas of the face.

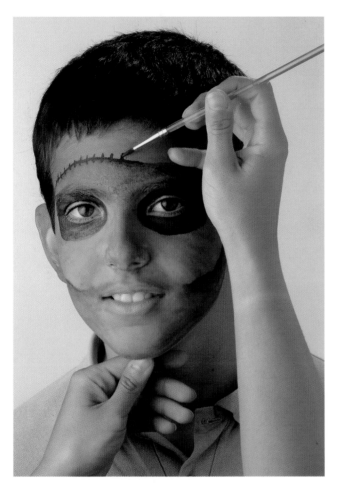

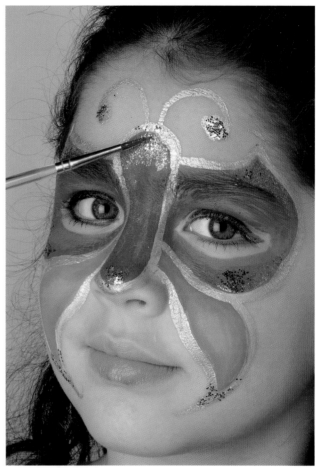

## Painting Details

Costume makeup often has small details that require a steady, accurate hand. One trick is to anchor the brush hand by lightly resting your baby finger on the face. You can also hold the model's face briefly when you come to a tricky bit. Always respect your model's comfort, and be courteous and gentle.

## Applying Glitter

Many makeup designs look more glamorous with glitter. Ready-made glitter gel for body and face painting is available and easy to apply with a paintbrush. If you would like a thicker application of glitter, you can make your own by adding glitter powder to hair gel.

# Body

# Art

Why stop at painting your face? Take your new skills to the next level with these fun body painting ideas!

# Stegosaurus

Turn your hand into a prehistoric dinosaur with fingers for armored plates!

**1.** Using the green body crayon, paint your fingers and the back of your hand green. Draw two little feet going down your wrist.

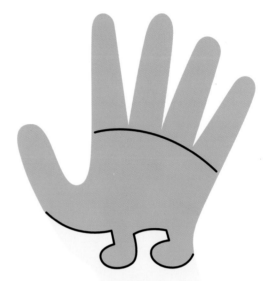

**2.** Draw a black line at the base of your fingers for the dino's back, and outline the feet with black.

**3.** Next decorate the dinosaur's "spikes" with blue crayon, and draw a smile onto your thumb where your knuckle is.

**4.** Finish up by painting some blue spots onto the back of your hand. You can give your dino googly eyes, or draw on some eyes with white and black.

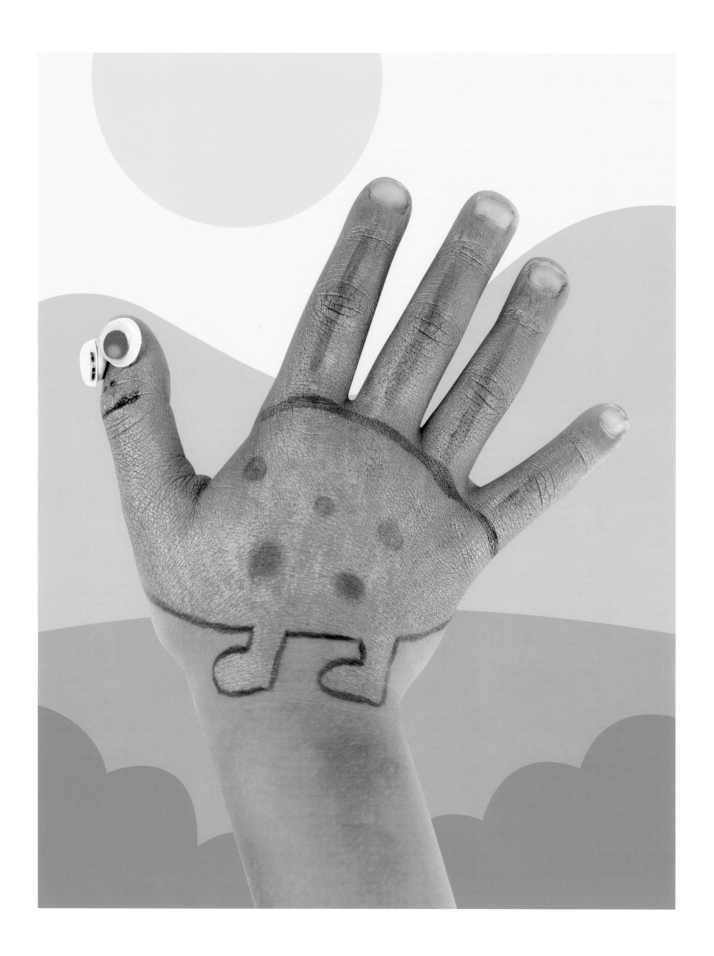

# Fish Fingers

Paint this cute fish, then try wiggling your hand to make it look like your fish is swimming!

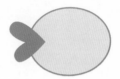

**1.** Draw an oval in the middle of the back of your hand using a silver body crayon.

**2.** Outline the oval in blue, and give your fish some big puckered lips.

**3.** Draw in some fins and a tail so your fish can swim super fast!

**4.** Give your fish some personality by using black to draw on some scales, and adding a googly eye, or painting one on with white and black.

# Bling's the Thing

This is a fun idea for some everyday color and sparkle. Get together with some friends and create original jewelry designs for each other. Using body crayons means that you can add lots of detail to your creations.

**To Make the Watch:**

**To Make the Bracelet:**

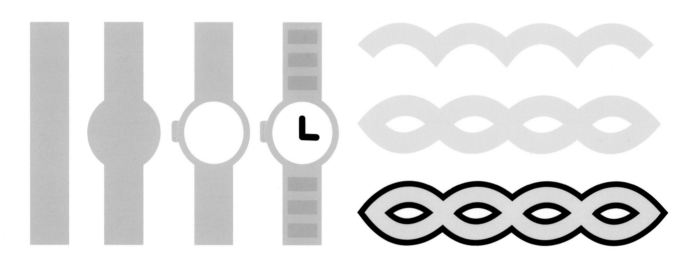

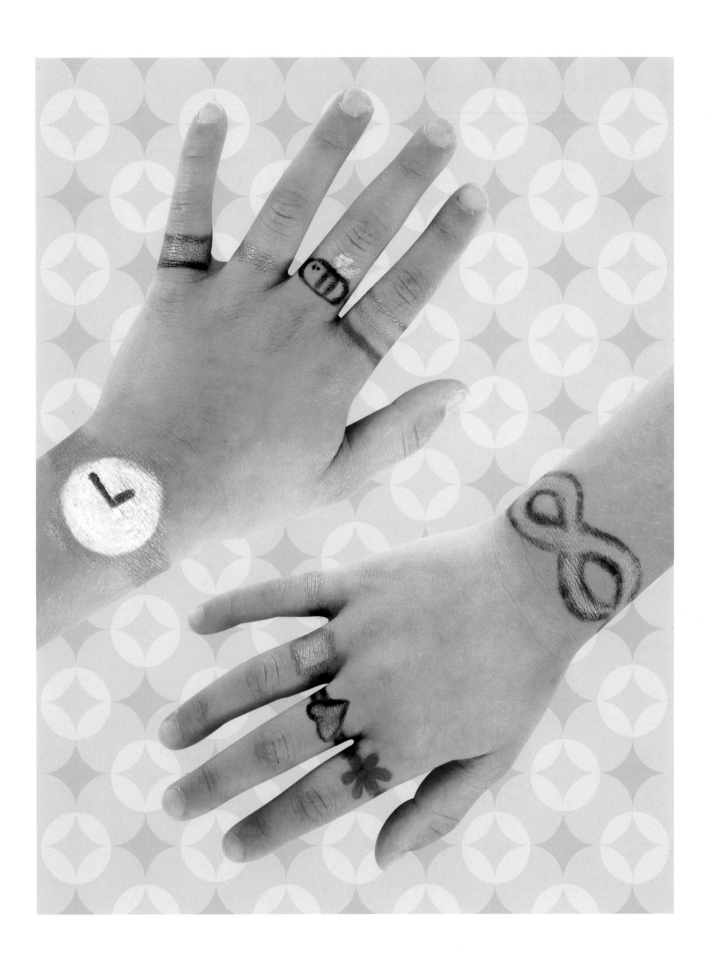

# Pendant & Pearls

Painting on your own jewelry is easy and fun, and you can use any colors and styles you want to match your favorite outfits!

**1.** Draw a large teardrop shape below your neck with a purple body crayon. You can place it lower if you want the necklace to be longer.

**2.** Next draw beads going from the top of the teardrop shape and around your neck. It's a good idea to get a parent or friend help you draw on the back of your neck.

**3.** Color in your beads with pretty colors. Think about the outfit you're wearing and use colors that match.

**4.** Finally, color in the big teardrop pendant. We used two different colors, to make it pop, but you can try any design you like. Fabulous!

# More Body Art Ideas

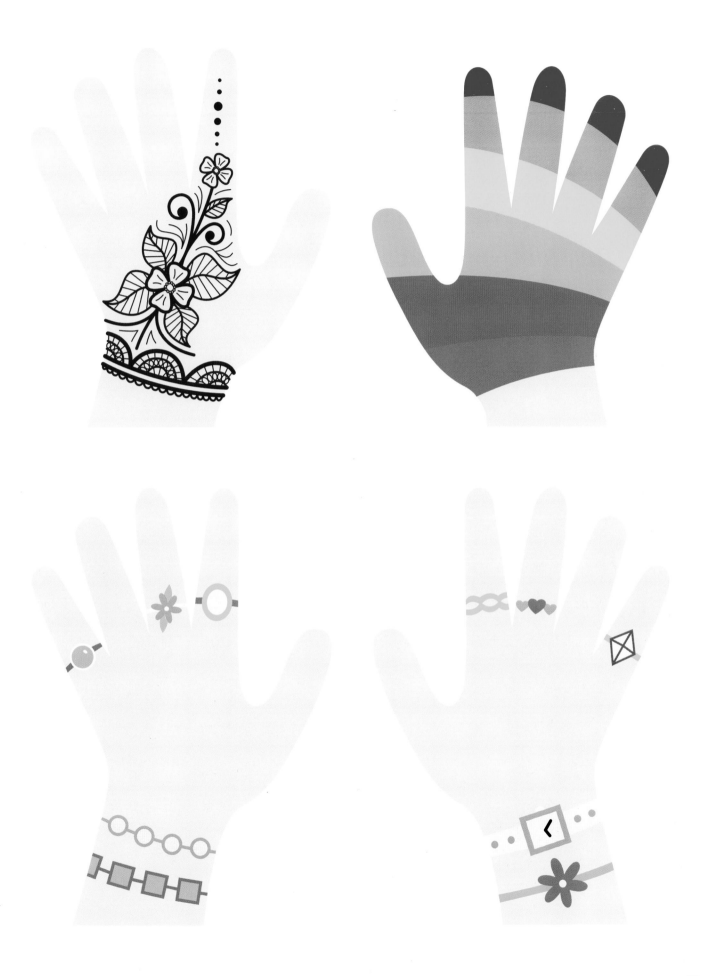

# Temporary Tattoos

We've included some awesome temporary tattoos in this kit so you can stick on some cool designs anytime, without scaring your mom!

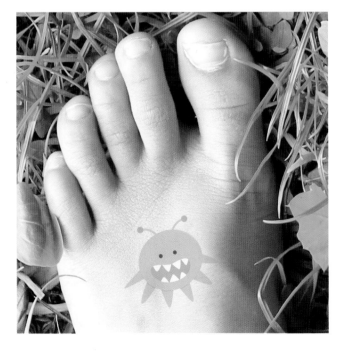
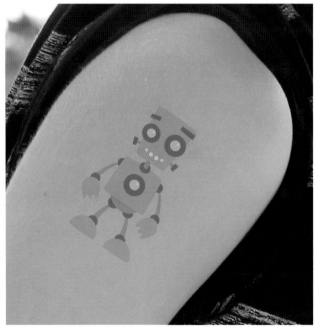

# How To Use Your Temporary Tattoos

1. Pick a tattoo you like and cut it out from the sheet.

2. Decide where you want to stick the tattoo and make sure your skin is clean and dry.

3. Peel off the clear plastic that covers the image.

4. Place the tattoo with the colored side on your skin. Even better, have a friend hold it down for you.

5. Run a cloth under the tap and wring it out so it's damp but not soaked. Firmly press the cloth over the tattoo.

6. Keep pressing the cloth over the tattoo for 60 seconds. Try not to move around too much.

7. Remove the cloth. Take a corner of the paper and very carefully peel a little bit off. If the tattoo isn't stuck to your skin yet, put the paper back and hold the damp cloth over it for another 30 seconds. If the tattoo is sticking to your skin then you can peel off the rest of the paper.

8. Wait a few minutes for the tattoo to dry before touching it or stretching the skin around it.

**Now show off your new "ink"!**